Date Due

Jun 23 '79		
No 16'79		
Aug 15 '80		
Sep 4 '8		
Ag 9 '8		
De 4 8		
NOV 21		
FEB 4		
DE 14		
APR 19		
JUL 19		
DE 6		

OLD NEW BRUNSWICK
A Victorian Portrait

OLD NEW BRUNSWICK
A Victorian Portrait

Photographs selected by Richard Vroom
Introduction by Arthur Doyle

Toronto / Oxford / New York
OXFORD UNIVERSITY PRESS
1978

ACKNOWLEDGEMENTS

I wish to express my gratitude to the Provincial Archives of New Brunswick and to the New Brunswick Museum for allowing me to use a great many of the photographs in this book. I am also most grateful to Mr. Robert Fellows at the Provincial Archives for the time he spent assisting me. At the New Brunswick Museum I am particularly indebted to Mrs. M. Robertson for allowing me to use photographs from the W.F. Ganong Collection, and for helping me research material for the captions.

Finally, I would like to dedicate this book to my parents, Dr. Alan and Clare Vroom, for their love and encouragement in my endeavours.   RV

Canadian Cataloguing in Publication Data

Vroom, Richard, 1943-
Old New Brunswick

ISBN 0-19-540293-6

1. New Brunswick — Description and travel —
1850-1900 — Views.* I. Doyle, Arthur T., 1938-
II. Title.

FC2467.3.V76   917.15′00222   C78-001560-6
F1042.V76

© Oxford University Press 1978
ISBN 0-19-540293-6
Printed in Canada by
T.H. BEST PRINTING COMPANY LIMITED

Preface

It is the intention of this book to show some of the best photographs made in New Brunswick during the period 1860 to 1918 and to convey as well the way photographers looked at their environment. Photography was first practised in New Brunswick long before 1860. Portrait studios began to open up in Saint John during the 1840s: the first, operated by J.S. Clow, opened in 1842, and there were four more studios by 1857. The technique used in portrait making was that of Louis Daguerre. The subject was required to sit motionless in strong sunlight for five to six minutes; then the plate was removed from the camera, developed in mercury vapour, and fixed in hyposulfite. When it was washed and dried, it was placed under glass to protect the image. This glass plate—a unique positive image — was given to the customer in a fancy setting.

The daguerreotype reigned supreme throughout North America for over fifteen years. In the 1850s the demand for cheap portraits became so great that the daguerreotypists could hardly keep up. In 1851 Frederick Scott Archer invented the wet collodion process, which was to take over completely from the daguerreotype because its increased speed, or sensitivity to light, made exposure time shorter and it offered greater gradations in tone and supurb detail. Most important, it produced a negative from which many prints could be made.

Photographers began making their own wet plates in the following manner. A piece of glass was placed in a vice and thoroughly cleaned and polished. Then the glass was coated with collodion (to which iodide and often bromide had been added). In the subdued orange light of a darkroom the coated plate, while tacky, was excited or made light sensitive by soaking it for five minutes in a bath of silver nitrate. When creamy yellow it was taken out, drained, and put still wet into a light-tight holder. The camera lens was covered, the subject was put in place, the plate holder was inserted into the camera and its slide removed. Then the lens cover was removed for a count of one . . . two . . . three . . . four . . . five . . . six. The lens was covered, the plate was removed, and over its surface a solution of pyrogallic acid was poured. In seconds the image would appear, increasing in brilliance. When judged fully developed, the plate was rinsed and hypo was poured over the plate to dissolve the remaining unaltered silver·salts. After washing, the plate was dried over a gentle flame and, while still warm, it was varnished. This technique was used by most New Brunswick photographers of the 1860s. It was not until 1871 that a dry collodian process was invented. By the 1880s, England was exporting dry plates and photographers in New Brunswick were quick to adopt this process. By 1900 dry plates were so sensitive that in good light an exposure time of a sixtieth of a second was possible.

Of what remains of the work of nineteenth-century New Brunswick photographers, the most significant collections are those of G.T. Taylor and Isaac Erb. They have remained intact—though the negatives have deteriorated somewhat over the years—and are among the most informative links to our past. Other notable collections exist of the works of William Notman, J.Y. Mersereau, and Olé Larsen.

George Thomas Taylor was one of the first Canadian photographers to take the camera from the confines of the studio to the outdoors, in his case the vast back rivers of New Brunswick. He was born on 6 October 1838, a year after Daguerre had produced his first successful daguerreotype. Taylor began his photographic career in 1856, learning from David Lawrence, a portrait photographer in Fredericton. Through an association with English officers in garrison, he borrowed and read English periodicals on photography, then built his own camera. (He built every camera and piece of equipment he ever used.) He was making daguerreotypes as early as 1856, and his handmade wet plates from the 1860s—of which his photographs on the Tobique River are some of the best examples — are still intact in the New Brunswick Provincial Archives. When dry plates came into use in the late 1870s, Taylor was quick to adopt them.

Taylor's surviving glass negatives are largely of landscapes, taken throughout the province, though there are many Fredericton scenes. In 1862 he had a portrait business in Fredericton, where he operated a 'likeness saloon'. However, the artist in him revolted against wooden likenesses, devoid of character. He was lured outdoors by the great rivers of New Brunswick, where his fellow Frederictonians hunted, fished, and explored. With his Indian guides, and his heavy camera and even heavier box of glass plates, Taylor ranged throughout the province, going from the headwaters of the Tobique River to the Green River near Edmunston, up the Restigouche River, the Miramichi, and along the Saint John. He even went into remote Squatook Lake in eastern Quebec. His last major field trip to the head of the Tobique River was made in 1906, when he was in his sixty-eighth year. Very soon after, Eastman Kodak made everyone an amateur photographer, so Taylor turned to painting. He died in Fredericton on 5 April 1913. His collection of glass negatives was purchased by the late Lord Beaverbrook and is now in the Beaverbrook Photographic Collection of the New Brunswick Provincial Archives.

The other major collection remaining is that of Isaac Erb, who was born at Kars, about forty miles from Saint John, on 30 May 1846. In the late 1870s Erb set up his photographic studio at 13 Charlotte St., Saint John. His forte was what would now be called industrial photography, in which he was a pioneer. Working extensively throughout New Brunswick, Nova Scotia, and Maine, he built a flourishing business, undertaking commissions to photograph factories, shipyards, lumberyards, and stores, and in the process creating a valuable and beautiful record of the development of our province in terms of the struggling business world. (This work includes some of the finest early interior photographs. Many were taken with natural light, but Erb also lighted his interiors with an early flash unit by igniting a measured amount of flash powder against a reflector by means of a spirit lamp.) Erb also recorded the life of immigrants from the time they left the boats: the surroundings in which they settled, their work, and the towns and cities they built.

In his earliest photography Erb made 'tintypes' which gave a positive image on a thin sheet of metal. These were $2^{1}/4''$ by $4''$, with his logo printed at the bottom and on the back. (Some of them were sepia toned.) He quickly changed, however, to the $8\frac{1}{2}''$-by-$6\frac{1}{2}''$ Eastman 'Stanley' plates, which had a light sensitivity of 8 ASA. These he used almost exclusively throughout his career.

When Erb died, on 13 May 1924, his business was carried on by his son John, who had been working with him. However, John's business gradually slid downhill over the next fifteen years. On his death in 1939 his widow put the studio and contents up for sale and it was purchased by Lewis Wilson, who acquired Erb's approximately 4,000 glass plate negatives.

As Saint John was the industrial centre of New Brunswick, it was endowed with a number of good photographers in the late nineteenth century. The studio of James Notman — brother of the famous William Notman of Montreal — was prominent. The city directories indicate that James Notman had a studio at 38 Prince William St. from 1872 to 1877; and, from 1878 to 1889, in the Ritchie Building at 54 Princess St. Few of the works of James Notman have been found, but New Brunswick photographs by William, who visited Saint John, include fine studies of the waterfront.

Little information has been kept on the lives of other early photographers. J.Y. Mersereau of Newcastle was a police magistrate who was known as '6 days Mersereau' for giving short sentences to the locals. Photography was a sideline at which he became very proficient. His photographs of the local industry and activities show he was a true master of the art in the late nineteenth century.

Olé Larsen, many of whose glass plates are now in the Provincial Archives of New Brunswick, was reputed to have jumped ship from Europe when it landed in the Newcastle area. He eventually had a studio for a short time in Newcastle near the town square, but remained quite poor. One of his proudest possessions was his horse, which took him around the Chatham-Newcastle area to do his photography. A few people around Newcastle can recall the white-haired photographer on his rounds about 1900, but no one seems to know what became of him.

Father Joseph Courtois, a Eudist priest at the monastery at Caraquet, was another New Brunswicker who made a significant contribution to photography, even though this was not his main profession. His work along the Acadian coast from about 1900 to 1915 provides one of our best links with the past in this area. He photographed not only religious ceremonies and his fellow priests, but also the fishing industry and the everyday life of the people.

The photographs selected for this book were drawn from approximately 20,000 that remain from this period. Besides the New Brunswick provincial collections, numerous private collections throughout the province were viewed, along with the Notman Collection in Montreal and the Public Archives in Ottawa. The true importance of early photography and the need to care for early collections is only beginning to be felt. It is hoped that this book will inspire others to research, collect, and preserve our past as it is revealed — often with memorable clarity — in early photographs.   RV

Introduction

THE FRUITS OF THE FOREST

The Saint John River Valley was settled after 1760 by Acadians, New Englanders, and, in 1783, by Loyalist immigrants. The Province of New Brunswick was created in 1784. For the first few years the settlers struggled for bare survival; their hardships became legendary during dreadful winters and back-breaking summers. Then they found an enormous British market for their vast timber resources. A boom began, and before long it permeated almost every area of the colony as Britain consumed ever-increasing quantities of the province's wood for sailing masts and lumber. Then came shipbuilding and a growing wave of immigration. Particularly numerous were the Irish, but many English and Scots also came to the province. In the half-century after 1825 Saint John and a dozen other towns built nearly six thousand ships to sail the globe. The shipbuilding and lumber industries, which were at their zenith in the 1850s and 1860s, put New Brunswick, and particularly the port of Saint John, on the economic map of the world. For three decades Saint John launched an average of over two new ships every week. It dominated the merchant-marine fleet of the Maritime Provinces, which was exceeded in size only by the similar fleets of Britain, the United States, and Germany.

But this prosperity continued for less than a decade after Confederation. In the mid-1870s the shipping world began to convert from wooden to steel ships. Simultaneously, markets for lumber products shrank in the wake of a world-wide depression. In response to the federal government's 'national policy', new tariff barriers further compounded the plight of some export-oriented industries. Dozens of shipyards, sawmills, and factories closed, and the economy entered a period of stagnation. New Brunswickers, with the promises of Confederation still ringing in their ears, looked on Ottawa bitterly. Although national tariff policies fostered secondary manufacturing industries, the Confederation arrangement had reduced the provincial government's revenues by fifty per cent and added new burdens formerly assumed by the British government. When the Intercolonial Railway, touted at Confederation, was finally finished in 1876, it by-passed the Saint John River Valley in 'the national interest' — that is, for defence reasons. Throughout the period tens of thousands migrated to Western Canada and the United States, causing a significant depopulation of English-speaking rural New Brunswick.

Those who stayed wouldn't accept economic stagnation as a permanent condition. Politicians lobbied with the federal government for a Chignecto Canal, railways, freight subsidies, and more tariff changes; they even considered Maritime Union. They were particularly convinced that railways would solve their problem by opening up the markets of Central Canada, and the provincial government subsidized railway promoters until there were twenty-four railways and 2,000 miles of tracks — more per capita than in any other part of the world. The port of Saint John was not neglected. By 1895 the city had invested one million dollars in new port facilities, but there was no significant improvement in port business. Undaunted, local entrepreneurs, the city, and the federal government multiplied their efforts. Before the turn of the century these initiatives, and the booming national economy, were clearly having a positive effect on both the port of Saint John and the provincial economy. Conditions improved. Nevertheless, New Brunswick continued to see itself as a stagnant economic backwater on the periphery of a booming continent—a forgotten society. Before, it was a successful offspring of the British Empire; now it was a poor cousin in a new nation.

Throughout the nineteenth century, when lumbering served as the foundation of the province's economy, it is estimated that seventy-five per cent of the population depended on that industry directly or indirectly. Most villages and towns could boast of at least one sawmill producing boards, planks, shingles, or lathes for export overseas or to the United States. For the most part these mills were fed with the lumber cut by hardy lumberjacks who, every fall, left towns and farms by the thousands to spend the winter in crudely constructed lumber camps. Most could not resist the promise of receiving $75 in hard cash the following spring, while being assured of their board for the long winter. Then, hopefully, they could earn more extra cash working on river log drive.

Wherever there was enough suitable forest land, one could find a lumber camp with a crew of perhaps 25 to 35 men. A typical camp consisted of a bunkhouse, where the men slept in double-decker bunks; a kitchen/dining cabin, where the cook was the undisputed authority; and a horse hovel. At one end of the bunkhouse there was a stone platform where an open fire raged every evening; above the fire was a great funnel-shaped log flue. Many of the larger camps had a company store, where men bought on credit tobacco, pipes, candy, underwear, mitts, and socks. In October the winter's supplies were brought in: salt herring, molasses, salt pork, barrels of beans and potatoes, oat meal, flour, and tea. Liquor was usually forbidden because of the potential disruptive effects of drinking — and the growing influence of the temperance movement.

The lumberjack's day began about 6:00 a.m. or earlier and he would be at the work-site by daybreak. A typical breakfast consisted of fried pork, moose or deer meat, porridge, beans, brown bread, and mince pie. A light noon lunch was brought to the work-site on a utility sled. Tea was made by filling a pot with a handful of loose tea and several handfuls of snow; the pot was then placed on an open fire. The work-day ended when darkness fell. After a hearty supper, similar to breakfast, the men sang songs, told stories, and played cards. By 9 o'clock most of them were asleep. At Christmas many of the men took a brief holiday to visit their families.

The lumber-camp season ended well before the spring thaw. With the long winter of back-breaking work behind them, and flush with hard cash, hundreds of lumberjacks descended upon otherwise quiet towns like Woodstock, Hartland, Perth, Grand Falls, Campbellton, Bathurst, Chatham, and Boiestown. Filled with rum, they harassed the shop owners, hotel keepers, and particularly the pretty girls. But before long things would settle down again. Piles of logs had been accumulating throughout the winter at the edges of the rivers or big streams, and with the spring thaw the logs tumbled into the water. Hundreds of lumberjacks again went to work guiding the great booms down the rivers and streams to the sawmills of the province. On the Saint John there was an annual 'Corporation Log Drive' when several lumber companies pooled their logs in one massive boom. Every spring the great log drives moved millions of logs down the rivers of New Brunswick, proclaiming the mightiest of the province's industries.

Shipyards were scattered along the North Shore and the Bay of Fundy coasts. At the peak of the industry, Saint John alone had twenty-five. Almost every trade was involved in building a ship. Working with a model, the shipwright supervised the laying of the blocks, the placing of the keel, then the stern and the stern post. As the weeks passed, one would see the great hull taking shape. When the completed hull was finally launched, with great excitement, there began the 'finishing' work of blacksmiths, carpenters, painters, rope and sail-makers, and riggers. As the new vessel left the harbour for overseas, it carried with it the legacy that ships built in New Brunswick held world records and were known in every major port around the globe.

NEW BRUNSWICK AT THE TURN OF THE CENTURY

In Saint John, sooty brick and stone buildings lean against each other in rows up and down muddy cobblestone streets carved out of the steep hills. Telegraph poles, joined by webs of wire, run up one block and down another where street cars, horses and wagons, and bicycles compete for space on congested streets. Fanning out from the King Square, landmarks, monuments, and buildings attest to the city's former stature as a leading world seaport. The main part of Saint John had been completely rebuilt after the devastating fire of 1877 almost totally destroyed its central core, leaving 13,000 homeless. Now, with the city rebuilt, King, Dock, Water, and Prince William Streets bustle with activity; in their buildings is conducted most of the important commerce in the province. The city can boast of an impressive variety of manufacturing enterprises, producing such things as axes, nuts and bolts, nails, skates, textiles, railway cars and locomotives, soaps, carriages, cigars, brushes, tools, and shoes.

The size of Saint John's population has not changed significantly since Confederation. Many of the well-to-do Loyalist decendants still live on Germain Street and around Queen Square and King Street East. (Others have moved to the suburb of Rothesay, where they have created an English village setting, with private schools and a common.) The city now has slums. They extend from the east end at St. Patricks and Erin Streets, named for the Irish who live there, to the north end on Main Street, down to Indiantown, where the riverboats dock. The port of Saint John — which acts as a doorway for about 25,000 European immigrants annually—is a seaport city in almost every sense of the word, with a 'red light district' and all. Dull wharf sheds, drab factories and founderies, old warehouses and continual fog give the entire city a depressing greyness.

In addition to carrying millions of tons of timber and lumber to Saint John for processing and exporting in the spring, the majestic Saint John River supports a thriving riverboat trade. Carrying passengers and freight from Saint John to Fredericton and Woodstock and back, thirty riverboats make regular return trips, some daily. Their cargoes include mail, farm implements, hardware, produce, molasses, and flour. These 'White River Palaces', as their promoters call them, carry as many as 50,000 passengers annually from Indiantown at Saint John to Fredericton. For many farm settlements the riverboat is their main contact with the outside world—the carrier of newspapers, mail and other news, as well as products otherwise unobtainable. Farm families look forward all summer to an excursion by riverboat to the exhibitions in Fredericton or Saint John; while for thousands of city dwellers the riverboat provides the only opportunity to discover the full beauty of the Saint John River Valley. The day-long cruises, carrying hundreds of passengers, are often accompanied by bands. Gay music and sing-songs help to while away the time, but for many the highlight of the trip comes at the noon luncheon, when they are served by waitresses in black dresses with white aprons and caps. At Indiantown in Saint John there are several hotels that thrive on this traffic: the Lorne, Ferris's, and Clarke's.

In all there are thirty-four riverboat stops on the 85-mile route from Saint John to Fredericton — at such settlements as Westfield, Brown's Flats, Hampstead, Oak Point, Gagetown, Jemseg, Oromocto, and Lincoln. A gravel road patiently winds its way along the riverside for ninety miles to the province's capital, a town of civil servants, merchants, lumbermen, teachers, lawyers, and clerks. In tone, in physical appearance, and socially, Fredericton is the crowning achievement of the Loyalist society's aspiration. The quiet blue river passes the well-spaced, dignified houses at its entrance — the homes of lumbermen, judges, and politicians. Adjacent to the riverbank parks stands the beautiful Christ Church Cathedral, a majestic symbol of the religious roots of New Brunswick's establishment. Close by, on Queen Street, stands the sombre limestone Parliament Building, adjoined by the government offices, where a few dozen civil servants unpretentiously conduct the government's business. A few hundred feet down this street stands the Queen, a hotel that for a few weeks each winter becomes home for most of the Liberal MLAs. Here, into the early hours of the morning, they gossip, plot, drink, and play cards. Another block down the street is the memorable Barker House—the boarding-house of Conservative politicians. As early as the 1850s legislators had coined the phrase 'Barker House conspiracies'.

Beyond Fredericton the river valley becomes more fertile and the farms more frequent. The river flows through the heartland of New Brunswick's Loyalist, Protestant farming community, passing the small towns of Woodstock and Hartland. Just before the river crosses the American border it forms a great waterfall. Here is the quiet town of Grand Falls, with its impressive broad main street, and at the northwestern tip of the province, beyond Grand Falls, is the larger town of Edmundston, almost completely French-speaking. Like the other valley towns, its economy is based on agriculture and lumbering.

Lying east and north from Edmundston for 125 miles a lonely, treacherous, muddy trail winds its way through the vast forest land of northern New Brunswick. Several miles separate each tiny roadside shack on the edge of the almost virgin wilderness. The trail ultimately leads to the new frontier towns of Campbellton and Dalhousie. As ports on the Bay of Chaleur, they are shipping centres for the vast quantities of lumber produced from the surrounding saw-mills. Their relative importance is increasing as lumber cutting pushes further north in the province. Fishing, too, is important.

Leaving Dalhousie, the lonely primitive road follows the coast of the Bay of Chaleur, the land of French-speaking Acadians. Here the Acadian Trail begins, and for mile after endless mile the road and the coast are separated by weather-worn log fences, and boxlike houses, grey and dull-white. Large families fish, hunt, and farm in peaceful monotony, just as their ancestors did when the Loyalists landed in the south. Every few miles stands a dignified Roman Catholic church, and beside it a comfortable rectory.

The road and the setting are interrupted by Bathurst, the only town of consequence in the Acadian northland. With its sawmills, it is busy and growing. Like Campbellton and Dalhousie, Bathurst is dominated by English-speaking businessmen. But rural Acadians in ever-increasing numbers, are being recruited to work in the expanding industries. Leaving Bathurst, the Acadian Trail continues to wind its way along the bleak fishing coast, not ending until it reaches the wharf at Shippigan beyond which, at the north eastern extremity of the province, are Shippigan and Miscou Islands, where a few hundred families live in even greater isolation.

In the winter the entire northern coast becomes a vast, windswept, frozen desert of snow. The roads disappear and the Acadian people hibernate with their families. Most of them have never been to Bathurst, their social contacts being their church congregation and the parish priest. When the long winter ends, they prepare for the next one by planting vegetables, cutting wood, fishing, and hunting.

Fifty miles below Bathurst, on the banks of the Miramichi River, are the old lumbering towns of Chatham and Newcastle, inhabited by the descendants of English and Irish settlers. Their impressive old public buildings and mansions bespeak an earlier more prosperous era. But the streets and waterfronts are still busily catering to rural shoppers and the lumber industry. The lumber mills employ several hundred; meanwhile some foundries and small factories continue to battle for survival. The J. B. Snowball Lumber Company is one of the area's largest employers, and its company store on Water Street permits employees to buy on credit until the men return from the woods to be paid for their work.

Along the Miramichi River, between Newcastle and Fredericton, the village of Boiestown still reigns as a great lumbering centre. It is dominated by the Richards Lumber Company and, like many other villages and towns, it is a jumping-off point every fall for the lumber crews working in the surrounding forest. In the spring, lumberjacks use the settlement as a base for seeking jobs on the great log drives. While waiting, they entertain themselves drinking rum and watching bare-knuckled fist fights. Because Boiestown is also an important stage-coach stopping point, the village is the site of the Avery Inn, a lively but 'high-class' hostelry. When the roads are good, a stage-coach leaving Fredericton at 8:00 a.m. can be in Boiestown in time for supper, but in bad winter storms the trip can take days. The snowdrifts and treacherous hills are among the worst to be found in the province. But the mail must go through, and often a sled, wagon, or horse must be 'borrowed' from a farm along the road, despite the protests of the farmer.

The road from Chatham winds down the eastern side of the province through dense woods and along the coast, where both Acadians and descendants of British settlers fish, farm, and work in the woods. Shediac, a substantial town surrounded by magnificent beaches, serves the neighbouring Acadian fishing industry. Thirty miles inland, on the muddy Peticodiac River, stands New Brunswick's third city, Moncton. Unlike the rest of the province, it is new and growing, a frontier town. It has become the commercial centre for (and at the expense of) the old Loyalist communities within a twenty-five-mile radius: Dorchester, Sackville, Hillsboro, Salisbury, and Peticodiac. But Moncton's greatest impetus to growth came with the increased importance of railway transportation in the last quarter of the nineteenth century and its subsequent establishment as the major railway terminal and service centre in the Maritime Provinces. The city's muddy main street is lined with plank sidewalks and bisected by electric street-car tracks. Carriages and horse-drawn wagons are seen in abundance. A variety of secondary industries has added to the prosperity.

Southwest from Moncton, and beyond the quiet communities of Salisbury and Peticodiac, the dusty road cuts through the barren Anegance woods. Halfway to Saint John, nestled in a beautiful farming valley, is Sussex, the commercial centre of the farming County of Kings. Over a century before, Loyalists families had settled, as others had in the Saint John River Valley, on the county's rich farmland. By patience, hard work, and thrift they built a dairy-farming industry.

Heading westward from Saint John a muddy, narrow road weaves its way down the southern section of the province and into Charlotte County. Secondary roads frequently branch out and wind their way to fishermen's cottages on the Bay of Fundy coast. The road eventually passes the busy little town of St. George and its prosperous granite industry. Further along, on the seacoast, is the beautiful Loyalist town of St. Andrews—the scene of a magnificent railway hotel. With its booming shipbuilding days behind it, St. Andrews has become a popular summer-resort area.

On the American border, at the southwestern corner of the province, are the twin towns of St. Stephen and Milltown. St. Stephen's main street is busy. Wooden sidewalks protect pedestrians from the mud of the street and the electric street cars. The town is dominated by William Ganong's local business empire: a candy factory, fishing enterprises, soap, and real estate. Milltown is overshadowed by a massive textile mill, which has eight hundred employees.

In spite of economic difficulties, New Brunswick was a place of relative contentment and stability in the nineteenth century. It was an age when people held tenaciously to those values that had transformed the province from an uncivilized wildness a century before: hard work, thrift, self-reliance, respect for one's neighbour's property and rights, unquestioning faith in the Christian religion as they interpreted it, and loyalty to established institutions. Although it was a time when grim economic realities dominated people's working lives, there was nevertheless opportunity for most to enjoy simple forms of recreation: hunting and fishing in the forests, rivers, and streams, which abounded with game and fish; bicycling; speed skating; horseshoes; lawn tennis; riverboat cruises; community picnics; festivals; parades; fairs; and Saturday night dances. It was an age of peace, faith, and simple optimism.

New Brunswick has been left with a rich treasure of thousands of photographs depicting provincial life as it was in the late nineteenth century. This book contains a carefully selected collection of some of the best of these scenes. They present a panoramic view of a simple yet diverse society in an age steeped in those values that have given us our heritage.   AD

1　Saint John harbour. The tallest spire is that of Trinity Church. *Unknown*, n.d. NBM

2 Saint John harbour from Trinity Church, looking towards Carlton.
William Notman, 1870. Notman Photographic Archives, McCord Museum

3   Saint John harbour from Chubb's Corner on Prince William Street.
William Notman, 1870. Notman Photographic Archives, McCord Museum

4 (*left*) Saint John. Market slip at high tide.
Isaac Erb, c.1902. PA

5 Saint John. King Street. *Givan*, c.1885. NBM

6   Saint John. Stanley Street. *Isaac Erb*, 1902.   WS

7   Saint John. Reversing Falls Bridge. *William
Notman*, c. 1898. Notman Photographic
Archives, McCord Museum

8 Saint John. The ruins of the
Custom House on Prince William
Street after the fire of 1877. *G.F.
Simonson*, 1877. NBM

9 Saint John. The ruins from the lower cove after the fire of 1877, with the remains of Germain Street Baptist Church in the background. *G.F. Simonson*, 1877. NBM

10 Lancaster (Saint John). New Fairville School, which still stands at 74 Morris Street. *Unknown*, c.1900. NBM

11   Millidgeville (Saint John). Royal Kennebecasis Yacht Club, which still stands. *Isaac Erb*, c.1900. PA

12 Saint John. Launching of the *Ludlow*, a ferry that transported people across the harbour to the west side of the city between 1905 and 1930. *Unknown*, c.1905. NBM

13 Saint John. The opening day of the Allison Grounds. *Isaac Erb*, 1908. ws

14   West Saint John. *Isaac Erb*, c.1900. PA

15   South Bay Mill, near Saint John. *Unknown*, 1870s. NBM

16 West Saint John. A four-masted schooner, the *Dornfontein*, being built by the Marine Construction Company of Canada Ltd. She was captured and set on fire south of Grand Manan by a German submarine in the closing days of the First World War. Rebuilt, she again caught fire and sank on her maiden voyage in 1918. *Unknown*, 1917. NSM

17   Ship-building crew with a schooner under construction on the Bay of Fundy coast. *Unknown* c.1900. NBM

18   Saint John. Shipbuilders at Hilyard's
Shipyard at the foot of Simond Street. *Unknown*,
c.1905. NBM

19   (*right*) Saint John. Inside the hull of a
schooner under construction. *Isaac Erb*, 1918. WS

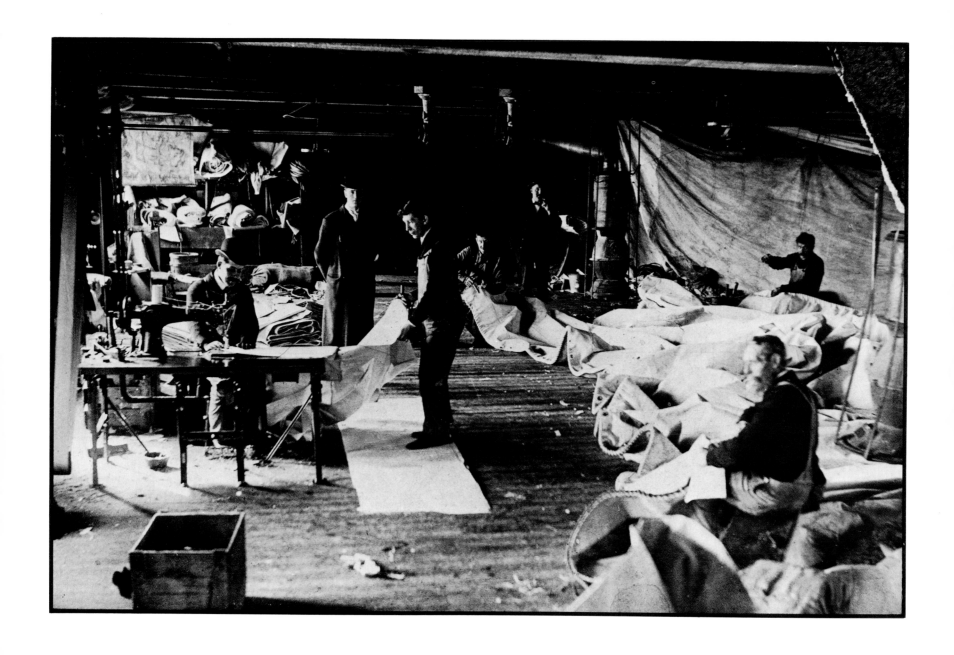

20   Saint John. Holder's sail loft, with Robert Wills at the sewing machine on the left. William H. Holder began making sails, tarpaulins, awnings, and deck chairs at 100 Water Street after the fire of 1877. *Unknown*, c.1900. NBM

21   Courtney Bay near East Saint John, showing
several types of ships under construction. *G.T.
Taylor*, c.1860. PA

22   Alma. Three-masted schooners at low tide.
R. Yeomans, 1880s. NBM

23   (*right*) The *Ada O. McIntyre* under full sail.
She was built in 1918 at Moss Glen, N.B.
Unknown, c.1918. NBM

24 (*left*) Moving logs by horse in the Miramichi area. The H on the logs is the mark for Ernest Hutchison, one of the lumber kings from Douglastown. *Olé Larsen*, 1890s. PA

25 Miramichi area. Hutchison's crew breaking a log jam. *Olé Larsen*, c.1890. PA

26 A Miramichi lumber camp almost buried in
snow. *Olé Larsen*, c.1898. PA

27 (*right*) On the main line of the Intercolonial Railway, between Newcastle
and Bartibog Station, white birch, used in making spools, is being loaded for
shipment to Britain. *Olé Larsen*, c.1885. PA

28   Miramichi area. Lumber-yard horses and their drivers. *J.Y. Mersereau*, 1890s. PA

29   Fredericton. Interior of the Aberdeen Saw Mill, which was destroyed by fire in August 1905. *Isaac Erb*, c.1900. PA

30   Northwest Bridge, near Newcastle. Square-rigged ships loading at Sinclair's Mill.   *Olé Larsen*, c.1890. PA

31 Boiestown. *G.T. Taylor*, 1870s. PA

32 Fredericton. Queen Street from Saint John Street. *G. T. Taylor*, c.1885. PA

33 Fredericton. Phoenix Square, with the City
Hall, from the Teachers' College. The loads of
hay are for sale. (The clouds were hand-painted
on the original negative by the photographer.)

All these buildings, along with the fence of the
Teachers' College, are still standing, though the
shops have been altered. *G.T. Taylor*, c.1875. PA

34 Fredericton. King Street, looking east from Westmorland. *G.T. Taylor*, 1890s. PA

35 (*right*) Fredericton. Residence of G. Clowes Brown, at the corner of Westmorland and Brunswick Streets. *G.T. Taylor*, 1886. PA

36 Fredericton. Queen Street,
looking west near York Street.
G.T. Taylor, c.1875. PA

37 (*right*) Fredericton.
Officers' Barracks, one of the
earliest buildings in the city
(c.1780). *G.T. Taylor*, c.1887. PA

38 Fredericton Fire Department No. 1 Hose Company, with their hand-pulled hose reel. The firemen from left to right are: Henry Pollack, Thomas Smith, Edward Segee, Jack Hersey, Nat Smith, Isaac Burden, Edward McGinn, Tapley McLaughlin, Jack McGinn. *G.T. Taylor*, 1887. PA

39 Fredericton. The original home of the Chestnut Canoe Company, on the south side of
King Street, just below Northumberland. It began business in 1897. *G.T. Taylor*, c.1900. PA

40 Fredericton. Hoegg's canning factory on King Street, between Northumberland and Smythe. The firm of D.W. Hoegg & Co. Ltd. operated during the last two decades of the nineteenth century. *G.T. Taylor*, 1880s. PA

41 Fredericton. This specially designed salesman's cart was made by Edgecombe's Carriage Factory about 1888 for the St. Croix Soap Manufacturing Company, St. Stephen, which marketed a white floating toilet soap under the 'Surprise' name, one of the largest-selling brand names in Canada. (See also plate 99.) *G.T. Taylor*, c.1888. PA

42 Saint John. Interior of the Waterbury and Rising shoe store. *Isaac Erb*, 1909. WS

43 Fredericton. A class in the Model School, which was behind the
Normal School building on Queen Street. *G.T. Taylor*, c.1886. PA

44 Moncton. D.R. Mills Confectionary on Main Street, between Wesley and Orange Lane.
Harry E. Mills and Roy Mills carried on their father's business until about 1970. *Unknown*, c.1913. MM

45 Miramichi area. Probably R.A. Jacobson, watchmaker, with his family. *Olé Larsen*, c.1905. PA

46 Chatham. This grocery store opened in the old Bank of Montreal building, Wellington Street, in 1897. *J.Y. Mersereau*, c.1897. PA

47 Chatham. Snowball's general store on Water Street, the company store for the J.B. Snowball Lumber Company, enabled employees' families to buy on credit until the men returned from the woods to be paid for their work. *J.Y. Mersereau*, c.1900. PA

48 (*left*) Newcastle. H.D. Peters' Drug Store. Charles M. Dickinson, who later owned a well-known drug store in Newcastle, is on the right. *Olé Larsen*, c.1900. PA

49 Bathurst. The carriage factory of Peter Elhatton. *Olé Larsen*, c.1893. PA

50 Napan (near Chatham). A typical
three-horse reaper, with the hay being gathered
by hand. *Olé Larsen*, c.1890. PA

51 Moores Mills. The stone picker of John N.
Fisk. *Unknown*, c.1880. NBM

52 St. Andrews area. Fishermen pulling up seine nets.
D. Will McKay, c.1890. Collection: Mrs. R. Haughn

53   Miramichi Bay. Net-fishing through ice. *J.Y. Mersereau*, 1890s. PA

54 Dalhousie. A branch fish plant of the Robin Collas Company Ltd. *Isaac Erb*, 1900-10. PA

55 Caraquet. Men gathering dried fish at the Robin Collas Company Ltd. *Olé Larsen*, c.1895. PA

56 'Boss' Gibson, New Brunswick's most prominent industrialist, and Fred B. Edgecombe, well-known Fredericton merchant, standing beside the railway engine, the *Fredericton*. In the background is the Fredericton Exhibition building, called the Crystal Palace. Opened in 1864, it stood at the corner of Westmorland and Saunders Streets until it was destroyed by fire in 1877. *G.T. Taylor*, 1869-77. PA

57 Fredericton Branch Railway
hand-car near Fredericton
Junction. Left to right: Fred
Nason, Steve Alexander, Alex
Mott, and S. Cormier. *Unknown*,
c.1887. C.W. Anderson

58 (*left*) St. George. The Shoreline Railway Station. *J.Y. Mersereau*, c.1890. PA

59 Moncton. Workers in the Intercolonial Railway car shop after it was rebuilt and mechanized in 1912. *Unknown*, c.1912. MM

60 (*left*) Rothesay. Belleview
Hotel. *Isaac Erb*, c.1900. PA

61 Newcastle. This majestic
residence was built by William A.
Hickson at 133 Pleasant Street in
1877. It still stands. *Olé Larsen*,
c.1900. PA

62 Chatham Head. The Sargent House, which still stands. *Olé Larsen*, 1890s. PA

63 Newcastle area. A 'staged' photograph, possibly taken at the time of Queen Victoria's Jubilee in 1897. *Olé Larsen*. PA

64   Fredericton area. The Roberts family, 18 August 1891. *G.T. Taylor*. PA

65   Miramichi area. *Olé Larsen*, c.1900. PA

66 Saint John area. The four men sculling are the famous Paris Crew of Saint John. They became celebrated when they won a race on the River Seine in 1867. In the world-championship race on the Kennebecasis River, near Saint John, on 23 August 1871, James Renforth, of the opposing Tyne Crew, was the champion oarsman for Great Britain. Near the finish he fell forward — from exhaustion, people thought — but he had died of a stroke, leaving the Paris Crew winners. The village three miles south of Rothesay called Chalet was later renamed Renforth in his memory. *Unknown*, c.1870. NBM

67   Saint John River. *G.T. Taylor*, 1890s. PA

68 Tobique River. Lieutenant Governor Gordon (in top hat) and party on a canoe trip. *G.T. Taylor*, 1862-6. GC

69 Garden's Creek Valley (Fredericton). A group of business men stopping for lunch while on a snowshoe tramp organized by W. T. Chestnut, who was interested in promoting outdoor activities. His company, besides manufacturing canoes, also made snowshoes. *G.T. Taylor*, c.1897. PA

70 Chatham. Ice-boating on the Miramichi
River. *J.Y. Mersereau*, 1890s. PA

71 (*right*) Fredericton. Queen Street. This is the Elwell Blue Nose Bicycle Tour, which cycled
from Grand Falls through Andover, Florenceville, and Westfield to Saint John in July 1886.
Lawson. Private collection.

72 Fredericton. 'Swampshum' Calder's boat house, which was operated by William Calder
for many years at the end of Westmorland Street. *G.T. Taylor*, 1890s. PA

73 Newcastle. Afternoon fishing at Buckley's Pond. *Olé Larsen*, 1890s. PA

74 Tabusintac area. Sportsmen with game birds sitting on a birch-bark canoe. In the centre is J. Rogers Lawlor and on the right is Jack Sargeant. *Olé Larsen*, 1890s. PA

75 Charlotte County. A hunting and recreational camp, with guests
and Indian guides and their families. *Unknown*, c.1900. NBM

76 Camp Comfort, on an island in the Saint John River above Fredericton. This is the second Camp Comfort, built on the site of the first after its destruction by the spring flood of 1887. Unfortunately this camp, and the island itself, were washed away in the flood of 1888. At the extreme left is Ernest L. Crewdson; Harry Chestnut is fourth from the left in a white shirt; Bill Chestnut sports white trousers; and Gus Tweedale sits farthest to the right. *G.T. Taylor*, 1887. PA

77 Fredericton area. Camp Comfort interior. *G.T. Taylor*, 1887. PA

78 Miramichi area. *Olé Larsen*, 1890. PA

79 (*right*) Gentlemen campers. A typical 'setup' shot of the 1880s. Left to right: John T. McKeen, Geo. F. Smith, Will Vroom, Mike McCarty (lying behind pot), Wellsly Peters (standing with stick), E. Ketchum, — Arnold (lying on ground), John H. Parks, Unknown. *Climo*, 1880s. NBM

80 Indians camping at the Blue Mountain bend
of the Tobique River. Their birch-bark canoe
forms part of their shelter. *G.T. Taylor*, c.1862. PA

81 Indian guides at the Narrows of the Tobique River. *G.T. Taylor*, 1860s. PA

82 Newcastle. ss *St. Nicholas* is at the wharf, and ss *St. George* has left it. The festive occasion is not known. *Olé Larsen*, c.1890. PA

83 (*right*) Newcastle. A picnic party leaving on the side-wheel steamer, the *Rustler*. *Olé Larsen*, c.1890. PA

84 Edmundston. A hand-poled ferry crosses the Saint John River, with an overhead cable to guide it. *Isaac Erb*, c.1900. PA

85   The steam boat is the *May Queen* (1869-1918) seen from Robertson's Point on the Saint John River. *Isaac Erb*, c.1900. PA

86 Maliseet Indians with the photographer's expedition on the Tobique River. *G.T. Taylor*, 1862. PA

87 The photographer's Indian guide. *G.T. Taylor*, c.1862. PA

88 Kingsclear. The Indian church on Corpus Christi Day. *G.T. Taylor*, c.1887. PA

89 (*right*) Kingsclear. Maliseet Indians celebrating Corpus Christi Day on the Saint John River. *G.T. Taylor*, c.1887. PA

90 Near Tobique Narrows.
Maliseet Indians of the Tobique
Reserve. *Unknown*, c.1905. NBM

91 (*right*) Near Fredericton. St. Mary's
Reserve. *G.T. Taylor*, c.1890. PA

92 A typical summer dwelling of the Maliseet Indians. The drying rack was possibly for dyed strips of ash used for basket weaving. *G.T. Taylor*, c.1890. PA

93 Near Fredericton. Building birch-bark canoes on St. Mary's Reserve (for which whites paid a pittance). When canvas canoes made their appearance with the opening of the Chestnut Canoe factory in 1897 (see plate 39), the building of bark canoes on the Saint John River virtually ceased. The Indian whittling the stick is Edward Paul. *G.T. Taylor*, c.1905. PA

94　The main street of Shediac. *Unknown*, c.1902. NBM

95 Newcastle. The business block along the town square, after reconstruction
following the fire of 1897. The photographer had his studio in the building at
the end of the row of trees. *Olé Larsen*, c.1900. PA

96 St. Andrews at the time of a campaign visit by John A. Macdonald during the federal election of 1887. Water Street. *Unknown*, c.1887. GC

97   St. Andrews. The Berry Block, at the corner of Water and William Streets, decorated for
the visit of Prince Arthur of Connaught. *D. Will McKay*, 1906. Collection: Mrs. R. Haughn

98 (*left*) St. Stephen. Water Street. Looking east from near the Custom House. *Isaac Erb*, c.1900. PA

99 St. Stephen. The original Surprise Soap factory complex. *Unknown*, c.1890. GC

100 Marysville. Boss Gibson's cotton mill, which began production in 1888 and became the largest single mill in Canada, employing approximately 500 people. The workers' houses along the river bank, called White Row, are mostly still standing. *G.T. Taylor*, 1890s. PA

101   Penniac Bridge over the Nashwaak River. *Geo. A. Burkhardt* , c.1890. NBM

102 Grand Falls about 1900. *Isaac Erb*. PA

103   Grand Falls. Broadway about 1900. *Isaac Erb*. PA

WALK YOUR HORSES AND SAVE A FINE OF $20.

1860.

104 Grand Falls. This bridge over the Saint John River stood from 1860 to 1914. *Isaac Erb*, c.1900. PA

105 (*right*) Grand Falls. *G.T. Taylor*, 1890s. PA

106 Madawaska region. Houses on the Saint John River. *G.T. Taylor*, 1890s. PA

107 (*right*) New Denmark. The Danish families coming to New Brunswick to settle all spent their first winter living together in this house in 1872. The next spring they began building their own homes. Notice the root cellar at the side of the house. *G.T. Taylor*, c.1872. GC

108   St. Basil, on the Saint John River. *Isaac Erb*, c.1900. PA

109   Edmundston. A panoramic view taken from Madawaska, Maine.
The open area on the left, on the far side of the Saint John River, is
now occupied by the Fraser Paper Mill. To the right is the mouth of
the Madawaska River; smoke is rising from the old Murchie Mill.
Isaac Erb, 1908. PA

110 (*left*) Restigouche River. *Unknown*. PAC

111 Campbellton. This lumber town, on
Chaleur Bay, had fourteen mills in 1910, when it
was destroyed by fire. *Isaac Erb*, c.1900. PA

112 (*left*) Campbellton. Aftermath of the fire of 1910, which may have started from a spark when it landed on a shed in Richard's Mill. Later, cinders fell into the lumber yard, setting fire to loose shingles, which a wind of gale force swirled over the entire town. *J.Y. Mersereau*, 1910. PA

113 Campbellton. Fire refugees on Water Street. The man with the beard is Hugh Marquis. Seated on the extreme left is Frank Foley, with Walter Jardine standing behind him. *J.Y. Mersereau*, 1910. PA

114 Campbellton area. McKenzie and Trueman's general store, with Abbie Comeau in the doorway. *J.Y. Mersereau*, 1910. PA

115 Dalhousie. *Isaac Erb*, c.1900. PA

116 (*left*) A cross-raising near
Caraquet, an Acadian village on
Chaleur Bay. *Father Joseph
Courtois*, c.1905. PA

117 The main street of Caraquet,
with the Eudist monastery in the
background. *Father Joseph
Courtois*, c.1905. PA

118 Caraquet. Unloading the catch. *Father Joseph Courtois*, c.1905. PA

119   Caraquet. *Father Joseph Courtois*, c.1905. PA

120 Caraquet. Poling a log raft. *Father Joseph Courtois*, c.1905. PA

121   Caraquet. Digging clams. *Father Joseph Courtois*, c.1905. PA

122 Caraquet. Fishing wharf, with herring drying on racks in foreground. *Father Joseph Courtois*, c.1905. GC

123 (*right*) Miscou Island. John MacDonald's fishing schooners off Miscou Light. *J.Y. Mersereau*, c.1900. PA